INTO THE MOURNING

A Handbook for a Grieving Parent

Dr. Tracy Kelly

Bruntzie Hill Press

ISBN-13: 9798436165929
ISBN-10: 1477123456

Cover design by: Art Painter
Library of Congress Control Number: 2018675309
Printed in the United States of America

"I dedicate this book to my son Hunter Jack Kelly. I am so proud of you my warrior. Your loving soul touched so many in your brief time here on earth, and you continue to touch us even in the loss of your physical being. Thank you for being my son. I consider it a wonderful gift from God that I was the one to be your mother.
I love you Hunterbug."

CONTENTS

PROLOGUE

Halfway down the trail to Hell,
In a shady meadow green
Are the souls of all dead troopers camped,
Near a good old-time canteen.
And this eternal resting place
Is known as Fiddler's Green.
Marching past, straight through to Hell
The Infantry are seen.
Accompanied by the Engineers,
Artillery and Marines,
For none but the shades of Cavalrymen
Dismount at Fiddler's Green.
Though some go curving down the trail
To seek a warmer scene.
No trooper ever gets to Hell Ere he's
emptied his canteen.
And so rides back to drink again
With friends at Fiddler's Green.
And so when man and horse go down
Beneath a saber keen,
Or in a roaring charge of fierce melee
You stop a bullet clean,
And the hostiles come to get your scalp,
Just empty your canteen,

And put your pistol to your head
And go to Fiddler's Green. (Author Unknown).

The first time I saw this poem was on a social media site shortly after learning that my son had been killed. I heard reference to it again at my son's military memorial at Fort Stewart Army base in Georgia, on September 9, 2015, on a hot and humid Wednesday afternoon. As I stood in the military chapel with high cathedral ceilings, surrounded by approximately 550 other service men and women and my two daughters, I numbly listened to three of my son's comrades talk about meeting again at Fiddler's Green. A prayer was recited by the military pastor, and my son's First Sergeant began to take role. One by one he shouted out the soldiers' names in my son's unit. The silence in the chapel was only broken by the sharp name of the soldier followed by the soldier's firm response that he was present. I waited on bated breath until First Sergeant called for my son. Not yet...not yet...but now...KELLY!...silence... HUNTER KELLY!...silence...HUNTER JACK KELLY!...a deafening silence that filled the entire room.

Suddenly gun shot was heard directly to my right and out the front of the chapel doors. The 21-gun salute, my body startled and jumped with each piercing shot. Taps followed the abruptness of the gunshot, played on the bugle, filled up the chapel, a message to the rest of the base that God is near, all is well, it is time to safely rest. I share the particulars of my own loss, to develop a portrayal, and set the tone for understanding the grief parents experience after losing their beloved child to death.

INTO THE MOURNING

A Handbook for a Grieving Parent

CHAPTER 1: ESTABLISHING A CONTEXT OF DEATH

What is death, but an absence of what once was. Death is always present, lurking around the corner, waiting, patiently, until its cue. It does not discriminate based on age, race, gender, profession, or religion. For some people, "death is the destroyer, for others it is a redeemer" (Leong, 2008, p. 149). Leong (2008) and Strang (2014) share that although humans live with the knowledge of death and dying from the moment they are born, they know little about it, which creates both fascination and fear.

Death is both a concept and an act, a universal fear, and a permanent alteration to an individual's world. A person's interpretation of death resides in all areas of a continuum ranging from the termination of personal existence to a continued journey of spiritual development either through reincarnation, or eternal life (Sage Publications &

Leong, 2008). The interpretation and perspective of death is also related to the manner in which death occurred. History shapes how death is understood and viewed, and these views change from generation to generation (Sage Publications & Leong, 2008).

Dating back to prehistoric times, people have constructed beliefs about what happens to their companions at and beyond death. Prehistoric humans have been found buried with stone tools and food, suggesting that they believed in existence beyond death, and that their loved ones would need such items (Peck & Bryant, 2009). As generations passed, and new ones took their place, death belief systems evolved and became more elaborate based on the culture. Religious beliefs offered life after death; Totemism suggested a spiritual link between humans and animals, plants, and nature; Asia, Egypt, and the Middle East expanded the knowledge about death and the afterlife; the Middle Ages brought Christians who shared knowledge on death preparation and achieving a good death; and for a while, death seemed tamed, natural, anticipated, and accepted (Peck & Bryant, 2009). Buddhists shared beliefs that death is nothing but another step in a person's journey, a closer step to the ultimate goal of enlightenment. Just as Christians refer to the Bible for how to live and die, Buddhists refer to *The Tibetan Book of the Dead* (Baldock, 2013) as a resource on how to maneuver through the afterlife. The book is often read to those preparing to die, or who are in the act of dying, to learn how to separate the soul from the physical body upon death, continue to move through realms of good and evil, and onto their next life (Baldock).

Impermanence is a foundational concept in the Buddhist studies, and death is viewed as an art, an opportunity to transcend from life to death to rebirth (Webb, 1997). Buddhism is similar to Christian beliefs in that life continues after death once the soul has maneuvered between heaven and hell, or good and evil. The understanding of impermanence can be helpful for navigating and coming to terms with loss, and help to develop a narrative about life and death.

The Civil war era brought great carnage to America, death was difficult to hide, and cultural views shifted. Approximately 620,000 American soldiers died, "equal to the total of all American fatalities in the Revolution, The War of 1812, the Mexican War, the Spanish-American War, World War I, World War II, and the Korean War" (Faust, 2008, p. xi). These numbers do not include the thousands of civilian lives that were also lost during the same war. Faust (2008) shares that in the midst of loss, death was culturally re-conceptualized. People clung to beliefs that death was only a temporary separation, not termination (Faust). The belief of eternity became the preoccupation, celebrating eternal life that accompanied death. Heaven offered peace and hope to families who were grieving. For families who could not wait to get to Heaven to see their loved ones, they turned to quicker methods. Spiritualism, described as contact with the spirit world offered the ability to communicate with the dead, through séances, mediums, and Ouija boards (Bryant, 2003; Faust, 2008). During this period, Mary Todd Lincoln regularly held séances at the White House to communicate with her deceased son Willie (Faust, 2008). People held close the belief that they were only separated from the deceased by a thin veil, and that their souls were infinite. For a population unfamiliar with death to this degree, with such significant amounts of death and loss, concerns and assumptions arose about how life should end and for who, when and where death should occur, and under what conditions (Faust). The Presbyterian Church warned Confederate soldiers that death is not merely an event, like birth, sickness, marriage, or illness, it is absolute and permanent, unchangeable (Faust). Death is a separation from what we hold dear to our hearts, of everything that gives meaning to life (Bryant, 2003).

As science and technology evolved during the 20th century, death became less tamed, and more feared. Americans sought new ways to cope with the thoughts of death, pushing acceptance and biological normalcy to the side in exchange for denial (Faust, 2008; Peck & Bryant, 2009). The topic of death became as taboo as the topic of pornography (Peck & Bryant). Even today the words *dead* or *death* are often substituted with other words such as *passed away* or *gone*. Both the United States and Western Europe obscured the idea of death, and also viewed mourning as indecent (Faust). The fear of not-being is so difficult to accept and provokes such extreme anxiety, that people attempt to distort or camouflage mortality (Bryant, 2008; Spellman, 2014). At times, these efforts at denial can result in pathological behavior, but for most, the minimization of the inevitable is an adaptive coping practice.

In the Handbook of Death and Dying (2003), Bryant explains Freud's views on the psyche. Freud theorized that when the fear of death increases, the libido decreases in the ego, and as a result, the ego drives anxiety into the unconscious (Bryant, 2003). The brain finds a way to protect itself from the fear;

yet, excessive use of defense mechanisms results in pathology and decreased life satisfaction (Bryant). Repressing, suppressing, and shoving aside typically leads to problems showing up in other places. Just as we attempt to push a beach ball under the water, it soon pops up out of the water in a different location.

Death awareness began to develop in the 1990's as topics related to death became more prevalent. For example, funeral homes began to offer services to help loved ones during their grief by offering counseling, education, and information; news and television programs began to focus on both death and dying; and government agencies began to notice the importance of supporting groups of people who had witnessed traumatic death by sending therapists and crisis counselors to treat the grief (Bryant, 2003). Hospice began to support the dying by helping ease their pain, and spirituality became a source of support for making meaning from death (Bryant, 2003). The focus of a good death, a dignified death, sprouted. As individuals were dying of AIDS and other disabling terminal diseases, concern arose for the welfare and wellbeing of these individuals as they deteriorated. Webb (1997) described people wanting to make a choice about the time for their death. Dr. Kevorkian, known for his medically assisted suicide, was in the headlines for helping terminally ill patient's rights to choose when and how their lives would end.

Still, the will to live is very strong. Most people do all that they can to prevent death, reject it, resist it, and shun it in an effort to lengthen life; yet, death is not failure. Death can arrive at any point in life, as an infant, a child, an adolescent, and adult, and to any person; priests, movie stars, mothers, fathers, siblings, kings, and soldiers. Each culture has its own perspectives about death.

Denial is one defense mechanism against death that is observed cross culturally in the acts of "preventing death, disposing of the dead, and helping make sense of death" (Bryant, 2003, p. 35). Still, billions of individuals throughout the world, from different cultures, societies, and political standpoints, arrange their lives around the principle and belief that beyond death is a reality more gratifying and satisfying than an individual can experience as human (Spellman, 2014). It is this belief that helps people through the massive weight of grief, that provides peace and comfort in the aftermath of loss, and the love and bond that death shatters (Spellman). Ernest Becker (1973), an anthropologist, shares that humans spend much of life fearing death, trying to avoid it, denying that in the end, it is the final destination to the end of a journey.

Ultimately, the act of dying is unique to every individual. Life when viewed as a journey for the soul, leaves opportunity to view death as an opportunity to complete the journey (Webb, 1997). As cited in Webb (1997) Dr. Elisabeth Kübler-Ross compared death to the metamorphosis the butterfly goes through when changing from a caterpillar, to a chrysalis, to a butterfly. At her Life, Death, and Transition workshop, she often used a toy caterpillar to demonstrate the life cycle of birth, life, and death (Webb, 1997). She compared life to the caterpillar, the body becoming ill and breaking down to the chrysalis stage, and death as the rebirthing of the beautiful and very different butterfly. When one views death from a place of fear, that our bodies are all that we really are, he or she cannot see death as change, an occasion for the spirit to move into a completely different plane (Webb, 1997).

Even with the death denial Americans exhibit, the culture paradoxically displays an intense obsession with death. Video games, movies, television, newspapers, comic books, music, and jokes abound on the topic of death (Bryant, 2003), and death is the most frequently presented topic in all of the mentioned venues (Abelman & Neuendorf, 1987; Mannino, 1997; Molitor & Sapolsky, 1993; Schecter & Everitt, 1997). It is also becoming an important subject matter within the field of mental health (Leong, 2008). Death anxiety is a central focus of therapy for many people, and is observed in many mental health disorders (Strang, 2014). Rollo May (1983) shares, "Anxiety is the state of the human being in the struggle against what would destroy his being" (p. 33). "Dying is an existential given" (Strang, 2014, p. 321). Irvin Yalom (1980) shares in his book *Existential Psychotherapy* death anxiety and fear as interchangeable words (Strang, 2014). Yalom further explains how the existential philosophers defined death anxiety; Kierkegaard described it as the "dread of non-being"; Heidegger as the "impossibility of further possibility"; Jaspers the "awareness of the fragility" of a person's being (as cited in Yalom, 1980, p. 42). We know about death, but we do not know about death. Yalom (1989) shares that while we know about death, the unconscious part of the mind protects us from the overwhelming anxiety and terror associated with death; yet, at times, these thoughts break through into the conscious part of the mind in full force, denial fails, and we are left to face the finiteness of our own and our loved one's human existence.

Because death is an act that all will partake,

a person wonders if the fear is an innate drive to survive, or a social construct. In Shultz's (1979) seminal article, it is argued that the fear of death is learned. To examine Shultz's theory, Lester (2015) shares a study performed with a group of 91 undergraduate students, between the ages of 18 and 25 years, who were in an abnormal psychology course. The students completed Templer's Death Anxiety Scale which measures for general fear of death, to assess the fear of death, and the fear of the dying process in both oneself and in others (Lester, 2015). The group consisted of 27 men and 64 women, and they received two versions of the test; a self-construal version (I, me, my), and an interdependent construal version (we, ours) to determine how they felt about items such as death of self, dying of self, death of others, and dying of others (Lester). The participants first read a paragraph about a visit to a city, with half of the group receiving a paragraph with personal singular pronouns, such as I and mine, and the other group receiving a paragraph with the plural pronouns, we and ours (Lester). The use of the pronouns was a priming before the individuals completed the Templer Death Anxiety Scale. The group that had read the singular pronoun paragraphs scored higher in fear of death of self, than those who received the plural pronoun priming (Lester). Next, the participants completed the revised Collett- Lester Fear of Death questionnaire which measures for fear of death of self, dying of self, death of others, and dying of others (Lester). The results indicated that the priming did not significantly alter an individual's fear of death, but that the fear is a steady trait (Lester).

Georgescu (2011) shared Freud's suggestion that a human's fear of death is an innate drive. Separate from the unconscious (Kahn & Liefooghe, 2014), Thanatos or "death drive" is the primal response to fearing death of self and of others, both psychological and emotional, and physical and biological (Georgescu, 2011; Tyson,1999). In addition, the death drive has a higher purpose, it is directed toward reaching a state of nirvana and nothingness (Kahn & Liefooghe, 2014). When a child is born and experiences a loving world, he or she develops a desire and will to live, to stay alive, that thwarts the death instinct (Bergmann, 2011). With so much emphasis, fear, avoidance, denial, anxiety, and uncertainty around death, it is not surprising to see the psychological effects the event has both before, during, and after the process. As cited in Gerogescu (2011) Freud explained that the death drive is a fundamental force in life, it affects and influences life, and drives people to seek pleasure and constancy.

During the Civil War, the experience of death changed for America. Between combat, disease, and illness, many soldiers died, causing almost every family in America to be touched by loss. As soldiers joined the fight, they became more prepared to die than to kill, accepting that they would most likely die away from their homes and their loved ones (Faust, 2008). Close friends and comrades took on the responsibility of informing family members of their loved one's death. Soldiers often carried with them a final letter to their families, saying their goodbyes in the case of their demise. Because of the suddenness of death most soldiers faced, it became more difficult to ensure a peaceful and good deathbed experience, resulting in a threat to what was previously determined as the correct way to die (Faust). The uncertainty and inability to plan for death, did not allow families or victims to prepare. Faust (2008) shares Reverend Alexander Twombly's sermon that even though at times death appears to be sudden and unexpected, it is not unexpected to God. Sudden death does not exist with God, as he knows exactly how long he intends the human life to be, and he has a course of action for when he plans on taking every soul home to him (Faust, 2008). "A time to be born, and a time to die; a time to plant, and a time to pluck up what is planted;" (Ecclesiastes 3:2, ESV).

As death changed for America, so did people's perspectives about death. Perhaps death is so feared because of the pain that accompanies it. Death from illness, accident, homicide, or murder is associated with suffering and agony (Bryant, 2003). In such types of death, loved ones are left to handle feelings and thoughts surrounding the circumstances of the death, and assumptions that the deceased did not want to die and holds little if any responsibility for the death (Bryant). In the United States, approximately 320 people die each day to an unexpected or accidental happening making accidental death the leading cause of death (Bryant; Denney & He, 2014). In addition, the U.S. has the highest rate for homicide and murder; or the taking of a person's life by another (Bryant), and approximately 125 Americans die by suicide each day.

Human beings fear death. The Handbook of Death and Dying (Bryant, 2003) shares that humans do not want their lives to end, and parents do not want their children's lives to end. That fear drives parents and individuals to become overprotective of their loved ones, to purchase life insurance policies, to sometimes experience anxiety, depression, and other mental health disorders, to deny and hide from the idea of death, and to spend thousands of dollars a year to prevent the end of life, the nonbeing of self. Yet, as C. S. Lewis (2001) writes in *A Grief Observed*, "And this separation, I suppose, waits for all," (p. 9). Perspectives on death vary across cultures, religions, and spiritual beliefs. Western philosophical views include the infinity of the soul. Christianity supports that while the physical body ends in death, the goal of the soul is to reunite with God (Bryant, 2003; Oppy & Trakakis, 2014). Eastern philosophies, such as Brahman and Hindu speak about reincarnation; returning to life once again to fulfill and complete what was not attained during the previous life cycle (Bryant; Oppy & Trakakis). Belief systems offer hope in the face of hopelessness. A continuation of existence after physical life ends. The death of a child, as an infant, adolescent, or young adult, is perhaps one of the most difficult deaths. A physical, emotional, and psychological extension of the parent, the loss of a child can be considered a partial loss of the self (Hamama-Raz, Rosenfeld, & Buchbinder, 2010).

CHAPTER 2: DEATH OF A CHILD

The experience of losing a child to death is considered one of the most profound, excruciating, distressing, confusing, and permanently life changing events a parent will ever experience. Words alone cannot capture the depth of the pain. Thomson (2010) shares that losing a loved one is not only one of the most excruciating experiences a human will suffer, but it is also heart breaking to witness.

Do not judge the bereaved mother. She comes in many forms. She is breathing, but she is dying. She may look young, but inside she has become ancient. She smiles, but her heart sobs. She walks, she talks, she cooks, she cleans, she works, she is, but she is not, all at once. She is here, but part of her is elsewhere for eternity. (Author unknown).

Fortunately, not all parents must suffer through such trauma, but for those who do, the process is the most intensely, agonizing, and consuming phenomenon of a person's physical being. The loss of a child influences all aspects of a parent's life (Barrera et al., 2007), and the pain is more intense than is felt after the death of a parent or spouse (Fletcher, 2002; Seecharan et al., 2004). There is not a day that goes by that the parent does not feel the loss, the void, and the distance of his or her child. From the moment a child is born, parents feel an urgency to love, protect, nurture, guide, support, and teach their offspring the ways of the world, values, morals, and independence. Children provide parents with a sense of purpose and immortality, a future of hope in continuing the family (Bryant, 2003). The death alters the family permanently and for generations. Immense guilt develops in response to not being able to protect the child. The Handbook of Death and Dying (2003) shares six possible sources of parental guilt as identified by Margaret Shandor Miles and Alice Sterner Demi:

1. Death causation guilt results from parent's perception that they may have contributed to the child's death or that they failed to protect the child from the death (p. 881).

2. Illness-related guilt involves their belief that they did not behave in optimal ways in relation to the sick or dead child (p. 881).

3. Parental role guilt originally labeled as cultural role guilt, is related to the parent-child relationship before and at the time of child's death. Parents believe that they failed to fulfill the socially prescribed overall parent role, and now they have no opportunity to rectify their mistakes because the child is dead (p. 881).

4. Moral guilt stems from having an overly strict conscience or religious belief system that stresses guilt and punishment. The child's death is perceived as punishment for parent's wrong deeds (p. 881).

5. Survival guilt may result because a child's death does not fit in the expected normal life cycle events (p. 881).

6. Grief guilt relates to parents' perception of their actions at or after the time of child's death. This guilt may progress through three phases: (a) in relation to parents' emotional reaction at the time of death, (b) in relation to grief reactions during bereavement, and (c) in relation to the "recovery phase" when the grief intensity begins to decline (p. 881).

When a child dies, the parents are left with a sense of hopelessness, anger, and confusion, and struggle with making sense or meaning of the premature separation. Survivors exhibit agitation, anxiety, depression, and regrets of unfinished business (Worden, 2008). Regrets and sorrow that the child barely began to forge his or her way in the world, barely made an impact (Hastings, Musambira, & Hoover, 2007) left no descendants, did not get to experience the years of adulthood, independence, family, and aging.When a child dies from a violent death, the suddenness and the finality evoke even more intense suffering and distress (Lohan & Murphy, 2007; Worden, 2008) as the family does not have time to prepare for such an incongruent unexpected timeline of events (Bogensperger & Lueger-Schuster, 2014; Bryant, 2003; Hendrickson, 2009, Worden, 2008). Not only are parents deeply impacted by the loss, but the entire family experiences significant distress. Parents who are undergoing a violent death bereavement are 23% more likely to have marriage difficulties that result in separation or divorce, feel less attached to one another, and they fear additional loss (Lohan & Murphy, 2007). They yearn for information, details, and reasons for their child's death. A need to understand why, to find meaning (Peck & Bryant, 2009; Worden, 2008).

The loss is also experienced by surviving siblings and grandparents resulting in about 19% of the population having experienced this devastating loss (Seecharan et al., 2004). In a study by Hendrickson (2009), eight articles on parental mortality after child death were explored. Parent suicidal ideation and completed suicides were at an increased rate compared to the general population; however, increased risk of death from cancer, stroke, or myocardial infarction after the loss of a child was not confirmed in the study (Hendrickson, 2009). In addition, parent's psychological distress interferes with other parent-child relationships and bonding, increases depression, anxiety, obsessive-compulsiveness, somatization, psychoticism (Lohan & Murphy, 2007), changes in self-image, polarized worldview, emotional instability, self-destructiveness, decreased sexual intimacy, decreased self-esteem (Salakari, Kaunonen, & Aho, 2014), poor wellbeing, and more mental and physical health problems (Rogers et al., 2008). When the death is due to a criminal act, such as homicide or murder, families are also often involved with medical and legal agencies. Mourning occurs while at the same time, attempting to navigate through the criminal justice system, prepare for a trial, and seeking justice. Grieving and bereavement is often suspended for years as families await legal resolution. Some families feel additional victimization as they await for lengthy court cases to end (Worden, 2008). The delays can alter grieving and halt healing as people are focused on the details of the case and distracted from their mourning. If justice is served and the case is closed, people can often move on in their grieving (Worden).

While the parental reactions to the loss of a child are varied, much of the bereavement is similar (Bryant, 2003). Beverly Raphael (1994) describes the loss from a parent's perspective as loss of part of the self, loss of a pleasurable friend and companion, loss of a spring of love, loss of past generations, and of future descendants.

CHAPTER 3: GRIEF, BEREAVEMENT AND LOSS

Grief is the natural response to loss that includes a variety of emotions, behaviors, and beliefs. Bereavement is the condition the individual is in after the loss of a loved one (Barrera et al., 2007). Shepard (2005) identifies the seven principles of grief in a handbook for care providers on helping the grieving (p. 25):

Principle One: You cannot fix or cure grief.

Principle Two: There is no one right way to grieve.

Principle Three: There is no universal timetable for the grief journey.

Principle Four: Every loss is a multiple loss.

Principle Five: Change=Loss=Grief

Principle Six: We grieve old loss while grieving new loss.

Principle Seven: We grieve when a loss has occurred or is threatened.

Faust (2008) shares that Freud described the "work of mourning" (p. 2274) as the act of coming to grips with the reality of the loss, and withdrawing emotionally from the deceased. The inability to adapt and integrate the grief into a person's life, often results in additional maladaptive responses. For individuals who have lost a loved one to a sudden or violent death, the grief response has been reported as being more severe and of longer duration (Hendrickson, 2009; Ott, Lueger, Kelber, & Prigerson, 2007) including post-traumatic stress disorder (PTSD) symptoms, and depression

(Hendrickson). Parents report and research supports that the grief changes over time, but remains consistently throughout a person's life (Arnold, Gemma, & Cushman, 2005; Bryant, 2003; Hamama-Raz et al., 2010; Thomson, 2010). An individual must learn how to mourn.

During the Civil war when numerous soldiers and civilians were killed, families and friends struggled with understanding grief, as they lacked details of the death, and often they did not have their loved ones remains (Faust, 2008). Funeral sermons were helpful in teaching lessons on mourning, finding meaning, and offered hope of an afterlife and being reunited (Faust). Funerals still provide a source for sharing the importance of a loved one's life, yet too often the service is held while mourners are in a state of shock, and unable to reap the positive benefits the event is intended to provide. Worden (2008) shares that the funeral service can help make reality and finality of the loss, which helps surviving family members and friends move to the first grieving task. The deceased is honored by words, songs, poems, and shared memories. The service allows a space for survivors to talk about the deceased, draw on social support from one another, and reflect on the individual's life (Worden, 2008).

Worden (2008) explains that when the family is in a state of numbness, they do not reap the positive psychological benefits that they could if the service was held at a later time.

When children die before a parent, no matter the age, the event disrupts the natural order of the life cycle, the family structure, and leaves parents feeling guilt and as if they have failed protecting their child (Bogensperger & Lueger-Schuster, 2014; Hendrickson, 2008). The supplementary guilt intensifies and complicates the grief process, making the use of coping tools more difficult (Fletcher, 2002; Hasui & Kitamura, 2004). Societal expectations follow beliefs that parents should die before children. As a result, friends, family, health care givers, mental health care givers, and other support systems are uncertain of how to respond appropriately to meet grieving parent's needs (Davies, 2004; Fletcher, 2002). Support systems can tire of the ongoing grief, experience discomfort in the loss, and distance themselves from the unthinkable pain. As a result, parental grief intensifies and can increase the risk of developing other health problems (Hendrickson, 2009). As parents struggle to rebalance the family system after the loss of one of the members, they are also attempting to find a place for the grief, and resume normal obligations and responsibilities (Lohan & Murphy, 2007). Most parents never regain their pre-loss identity and sense of self (Arnold & Buschman Gemma, 2008; Malkinson, Rubin, & Witztum, 2006). The loss is so intense and traumatic, the parent is permanently altered. The attachment theory grief model helps to understand the parental state of mind after child loss.

Attachment Theory Grief Model

Attachment occurs during the first few years of life between infant and caregiver. The three types of attachment behavior are described as secure or autonomous, ambivalent-resistant or preoccupied, and avoidant or dismissing (Bowlby, 1988; Thomson, 2010). When the caregiver adequately meets the infant's needs, healthy attachment occurs (Bowlby, 1988; Vicedo, 2011). Deficient responses to the infant's needs often results in unhealthy, anxious, avoidant, and ambivalent attachment styles (Bowlby, 1988; Vicedo, 2011). Crying, laughter, hunger, and other behaviors elicit a response in the adult caregiver, reassuring their child that they are safe, heard, and understood. Infants grow up and reproduce these same attentive behaviors with their own offspring (Thomson, 2010). During threatening conditions, these attachment behaviors are activated in both the infant and the caregiver, including when there is a separation (Bowlby, 1988). When children are away from parents or caregivers, the parental psychological response is to protect, comfort, and provide safety (Thomson). This response does not end even in death. Thomson (2010) shares Bowlby's (1980) four stage mourning process that varies depending on the individuals attachment style: *numbness* and shock at understanding that their loved one will no longer move through the phases of development; *yearning and searching* for the deceased individual which is a natural activated attachment response due to the separation; *disorganization and disorientation* which could be further complicated by disorganized attachment styles; and *reorganization* which is indicated by less disorganized reactions. Thomson (2010) shares that successful grieving is not equivalent to recovery. Recovery suggests that the mourning parent will at some time return to his or her pre-loss functioning and self; yet, more realistically, grief is the effort to adapt to a very different life that includes the loss of the loved one (Thomson, 2010). This adaptation may or may not occur in stages. Bowlby's (1980) attachment theory model takes into account the bond between a parent and child, and recognizes and validates the significant bond that can develop between a child and a parent. There is not an expected linear process which allows for the bereaved to move fluidly through the differing responses to mourning.

Kübler-Ross Model

The grief model, as developed by Dr. Elisabeth Kübler-Ross, explained in Beyond the Five Stages of Grief (2011) is a commonly used framework to help clinicians, educators, physicians, psychologists, nurses, supervisors, and other individuals help people understand the grieving process. The model, which is deeply entrenched in western culture (Davis-Konigsberg, 2011), is a five-stage linear process that attempts to normalize the wide variety of thoughts and emotions a person experiences after losing a loved one (Beyond the Five Stages of Grief, 2011). The stages as defined by Kübler- Ross, seen in Figure 1, are denial, anger, bargaining, depression, and acceptance and are not limited to death, but can also apply to other loss such as divorce (Beyond the Five Stages of Grief, 2011).

Once Kubler-Ross shared her identification of five stages, people grapple with as they end life in 1969, *On Death and Dying,* practitioners quickly embraced the model and started to apply it to the grief an individual experiences when losing a loved one. Kubler-Ross did not originally intend for the model to apply someone else, but to a person facing his or her own death (Davis-Konigsberg, 2011). In 2005, Kubler-Ross did not object to the theory being used to include grieving others in her book, *On Grief and Grieving* (Davis-Konigsberg, 2011). When skeptics began to question the idea of stages in the 1970's Kubler-Ross agreed that the stages do not have to happen in sequence, and some steps might be skipped, and supporters of the Kubler- Ross model believe that she never intended the stages to be taken literally (Davis-Konisberg, 2011).

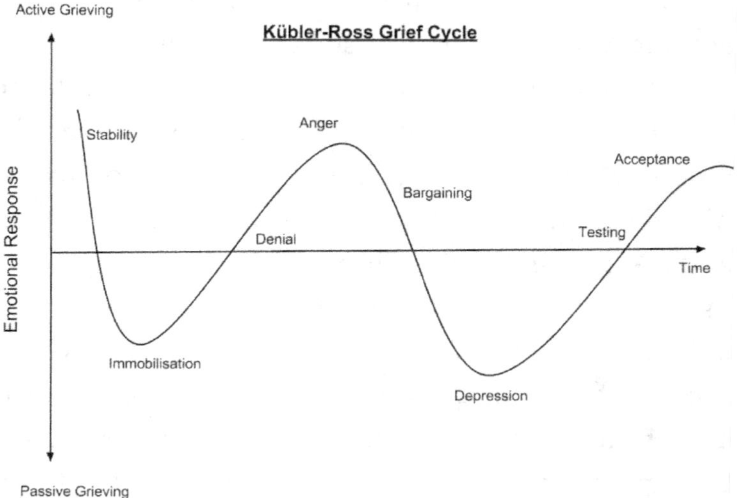

Figure 1. Kübler-Ross Grief Cycle. The figure suggests the five stages involved in the grieving process, also known as DABDA, which can be applied to any type of event that the individual experiences as life-changing (Retrieved from changingminds.org).

The model talks about the acceptance stage of grief. The word acceptance by itself implies that if this step does not occur, the individual is exhibiting a disordered and unnatural response. Accepting that a child has been taken from life, is beyond the ability of most parents. Understanding could be more appropriate. As the death becomes a reality, parents realize that life will never be the same, the grief lessens in intensity, and parents begin to become more engaged in their own lives again (Bryant, 2003; Rubin & Malkinson, 2001; Thomson, 2010). Acceptance comes from accepting that an individual will not recover from the experience; life will not return to how it was before the death (Arnold & Buschman Gemma, 2008; Elder, 1998; Malkinson et al., 2006; Sormanti & August, 1997; Thomson, 2010). Grief is a very individual experience. No two people will share the same feelings, thoughts, and loss in exactly the same way. Grief models provide a structure of how grief looks, they do not fully explain that individuals may enter, and re-enter, each stage, numerous times, sometimes within the same hour. With this in mind, Figure 2 could be a more accurate depiction of the grieving experience.

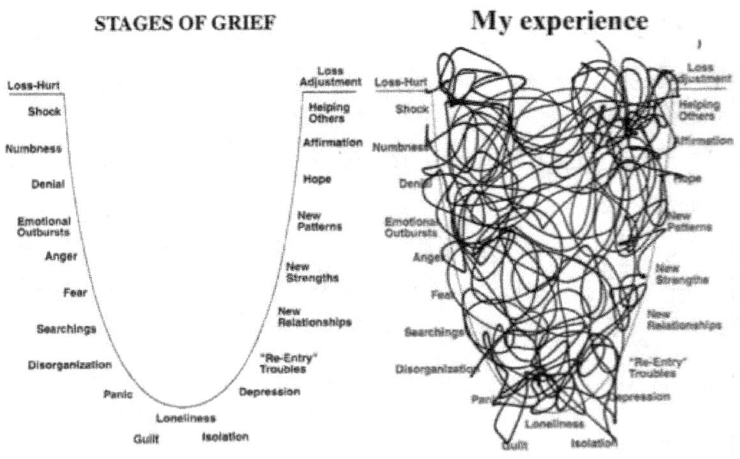

Figure 2. Stages of Grief. A more accurate representation of the grieving process.(Image retrieved fromhttp://sequencewiz.org/2015/11/20/leaning-into-the-sharp-points-how-yoga-can-help-with-the-grief-process/).

The Handbook of Death and Dying (Bryant, 2003) shares that the average amount of time for grief is between 12 and 18 months, with additional time expected when the death is that of a child. The DSM-5 suggest pathology, or persistent complex bereavement disorder, if after

12 months for adults after the death, and 6 months for children, the individual still experiences "severe grief reactions," (P. 792) and the person struggles with functioning (American Psychiatric Association, 2013). Severe reactions could include: Marked difficulty accepting the death, disbelief or emotional numbness over the loss, bitterness or anger related to the loss, excessive avoidance of reminders of the loss including situations, thoughts and feelings, difficulty with positive reminiscing about the deceased, a desire to die and be with the deceased, difficulty trusting others, feeling alone and detached from others, feeling that life is meaningless or empty, confusion about one's role in life, diminished sense of one's identity, difficulty or reluctance to pursue interests since the loss, and clinically significant distress or impairment in social, occupational, or other important areas of functioning. (p. 790). While most severe symptoms of grief might subside, they will often return again in full, sometimes triggered by special times of the year, but the underlying pain will sustain for the remainder of the parent's life (Bryant, 2003; Sormanti & August, 1997). The need and the drive to stay connected with the deceased, to keep him or her alive, to not let go, are normal responses to

the loss. Spirituality, prayer, meditation, storytelling, and faith are ways in which individuals try to gain understanding, meaning, keep the deceased immortal, cope, and heal.

Worden's Task Model

Worden's model, is similar to the Kübler-Ross model in that it describes grief as occurring in stages. The tasks that take place at each stage of the model are acceptance of the loss, working through the pain, adaptation to a new way of life, and finding ways to keep the connection with the person who has passed, while at the same time learning to live with the loss (Smit, 2015). Theorists have placed grief in a linear sequence of events, outlining how an individual progresses through the experience, and when the process is complete. Unfortunately, studies show that grief is not a linear nor a temporary event (Arnold et al., 2005; Bryant, 2003; Drenth, Herbst, & Strydom, 2010; Hamama-Raz et al., 2010; Thomson, 2010) and such thinking and expectations can pathologize grieving and bereavement. Even with the described stages, Worden (2008) also believed and remained flexible in that grief was not linear in process, and accepted that every individual mourns and revisits tasks as needed (Smit, 2015). Additional factors that influence the grieving process are the relationship and the attachment to the deceased, how the person died, whether the death was traumatic, violent, sudden, or unexpected, death by suicide, other losses, family history of mental health and unresolved grief, life experience, faith, coping styles, and beliefs about social support (Smit, 2015).

Continuing-Bond Model

Developed by Klass, Silverman, and Nickman, and explained in Smit (2015), loss through death is not viewed as permanent separation, but as a change, and continued connections are encouraged even after death. Similar to attachment theory, the bonds between loved ones are seen as persisting beyond death. The maintaining of these bonds are not seen as pathological in nature, but as natural as the person does not let go, but continually negotiates the meaning of the loss (Smit, 2015). While for some, relinquishing the bond is necessary for adjustment, for others, enhancing the connection is beneficial (Stroebe, Schut, & Boerner, 2010). Further research is warranted with the model to determine if the continuing nature of the bonds change throughout the grieving experience.

The Dual Process Model

Developed by Stroebe and Schut, (as cited in Smith, 2015) the dual-process model (DPM) recognizes the vacillation individuals go through during the grief encounter. As individuals attempt to cope with grief, they move from a loss-oriented response to a restoration-oriented response (Smit, 2015). Buglass (2010), Dent (2005), and Hall (2011) share that adequate time to grieve is necessary, with controlled expression of the feelings.

The loss-oriented response focuses on grief work around the loss and includes crying, separation, yearning, missing, and remembering the deceased (Drenth et al., 2010; Smit, 2015). The DPM is consistent with Bowlby's attachment theory grief model. The restoration-oriented response focuses on the external changes to the mourner's life (Drenth et al., 2010; Smit, 2015). New routines, specific problems, and ways to adapt to grief are explored as well as how to deal with adjusting to the loss, social isolation loneliness, and role changes (Drenth et al., 2010). One of the key characteristics of the DPM is the opportunity for the bereaved to take breaks from carrying on with life, dealing with the loss, and get back into it when he or she is ready (Drenth et al., 2010). Both Bowlby and the DPM models agree that pre-loss functioning is not the goal, but rather adapting to the loss, and the difference in life as a result of the loss (Drenth et al., 2010; Smit, 2015; Thompson, 2010). A limitation to the model is that clinicians and the bereaved do not have a structured model of how to determine if grief is complicated or uncomplicated, and therefore, may struggle with determining if the bereaved is healing.

CHAPTER 4: PHYSIOLOGICAL RESPONSE TO GRIEF

Outwardly, grief is universally observed as a natural response to loss. Crying, isolating, anguish in facial expressions, low energy, withdrawal, raging, moaning, and depressed mood are often expressions of grief and bereavement. Grief is a survival instinct. Shepard (2005) describes that when a human organism depends upon another for survival, it will act to reconnect when it is separated from that source. If the connection is not possible, then the being reacts with grief to the loss of the attachment (Shepard, 2005). Attachment behaviors are intended for survival. Through crying, protest, and distress, infants let their caregivers know they are in need. When caregivers respond an attachment bond develops (Bowlby, 1988).

The style of attachment influences the way

an individual grieves separation, illness, divorce, injury, and death (Shepard, 2005). Grief is conveyed through behaviors, thoughts, and feelings as well as psychologically, physically, socially, and spiritually (Shepard, 2005). Cognitive challenges include loss of interest in previous activities, loss of pleasure in sex, food, social events, memory loss and trouble with concentration, sluggishness, numbness, intrusive and disturbing thoughts and images about the loss, helplessness, confusion, hopelessness, thoughts and sounds of the loved ones voice, and mental fatigue (Shepard, 2005; Worden, 2008). Physically, the body also responds to the loss and often gives in to increased illness, disease, and even death. Because of the increased stress associated with trauma and loss, the body's immune system, heart, circulation, nerves, bones, muscles, hormones, senses, and viscera suffer (Shepard, 2005). Harmful habits are sometimes taken on or increased such as alcohol use, drugs, smoking cigarettes, and other risky behaviors. Shepard (2005) and Worden (2008) share that people often complain of dizziness, nausea, dryness in the throat, shortness of breath, tightness in the chest, chest pains, stomach aches, lack of energy, muscle aches, increased colds, loss or gain of weight, and sexual dysfunction.

Crying

Increased crying is an attachment response to the loss. Helpful as a way to bring the lost attachment figure close (Bowlby, 1988), crying also evokes a protective and caring reaction (Parkes & Weiss, 1983), and is potentially healing (Lutz, 1999; Worden, 2008). Some theorists believe that crying is "the most important pathway to mental health" (Lutz, 1999, p. 116). Researchers believe that as stress accumulates in the body, chemical imbalances increase. Whereas it is known that crying reduces emotional stress, researchers are investigating the content of tears shed during stressful times compared to tears shed from irritation (Worden, 2008). Some researchers suggest that crying in times of distress allows the body to return to homeostasis by removing toxic substances from the body that have accumulated due to stressful events (Worden, 2008). Tears allow individuals to clear up their "psychic house" (p. 118) to allow emotions to return to their place, or as Aristotle described, catharsis (Lutz, 1999). Both Hindu and Yiddish proverbs teach that tears help the complexion and make the heart lighter (Lutz).

Throughout cultures, and over time, tears have

represented different meanings. Some cry out of respect, some out of traditional practice, and some out of a sense of duty. Tear express messages to self and to others. Crying at a funeral takes place in every culture but one. Lutz (1999) shares that the U.S. State Department has identified Bali as a culture where crying takes place only at death, but not at the funeral, which takes place years after the death. Still crying is a universal human response to death (Lutz, 1999).

CHAPTER 5: SPIRITUALITY

Spirituality, faith, religion, meditation, after-death-comunication, and prayer are often methods to keep connected with the deceased and instill hope. For some cultures in particular, after death communication has historical and traditional importance. Native Americans welcome ancestral spirits as helpers and guides, the Chinese culture sees ancestor worship as a survival tool and use mediums to seek practical advice (Bryant, 2003), and Buddhist cultures regard death as part of a spiritual cycle (Sormanti & August, 1997). In American culture, such practices are not as revered, and death is viewed with finality (Sormanti & August, 1997). Western culture encourages an individual to move on, get over it, and let go of their loved ones (Sormanti & August, 1997); yet, faith and spiritual practices are very useful for some in integrating and resolving grief. In a study developed in London, participants were assessed to explore the relation that spiritual beliefs had on their bereavement. The results showed that over a 14 month period of time following a death, those individuals who had strong spiritual beliefs were able to resolve their grief; whereas, those with no spiritual beliefs had not resolved grief, in the same period of time (Walsh, King, Jones, Tookman, & Blizard, 2002). Parents who experienced after death spiritual experiences with their deceased children, such as visions, dreams, physical sensations, and premonitions, psychologically benefitted (Ganzevoort & Falkenburg, 2012; Sormanti & August, 1997).

Grief is best managed through integration of the death experience and the deceased into life, and lack of spiritual beliefs can complicate grief (Sormanti & August, 1997; Walsh et al., 2002). In studies with parents who have lost their children to death, numerous recounts of spiritual encounters with the deceased have been reported. After death communications (ADCs) include messages from those who have passed, voices, odors, visual images, dreams, the appearance of rainbows or animals, and other phenomena that are symbolic, and are considered normal grief reactions, and are not pathological responses (Kwilecki, 2011; Sormanti & August, 1997). From an attachment perspective, ongoing connection with the deceased is seen as a healthy coping means that addresses the secure attachment bonds while adjusting to the loss, and helps maintain the identity as a parent (Sormanti & August, 1997; Steffen & Coyle, 2010), as long as it does not prevent the parent from acknowledging the reality of the death (Field, 2008). ADC often consists of deceased loved ones offering comfort, reassurance, forgiveness, and peace. Kwikecki (2011) shares that some ADC can include hope that the loved one is dwelling with God, and are visiting only with God's intention and permission. Communications with the deceased can often encourage surviving family members to seek more spirituality, faith, and religion. Kwikecki (2011) reminds that the Bible scriptures offer reassurance that the soul is infinite and God has a plan that should be trusted. ADC is one way parents maintain their bonds with their deceased children. The grieving process is another way to stay connected. As grief begins to integrate into life, parents may seek other venues for honoring and keeping their child alive and remembered.

Keeping Connected

Music, song lyrics, poetry, photographs, stories, journaling, and art are methods of capturing moments in time, precious memories to pass down to the next generations to come. The Bible is an example of stories that have been handed down from generation to generation, providing morals, values, and guidelines from which to live. Musicians and artists also pass down music, lyrics, and art that influence others in a variety of ways; storytellers of love, loss, hope, despair, tragedy, passion, freedom, persecution, life, and death. Recalling a past loved one's presence in the world through favorite songs, music, photos, and videos creates meaningful connections. All of these evoke emotional and physical responses. Music is related to cognitive development, mood, intellectual development, social connection (Southgate & Roscigno, 2009) and is helpful in soothing, regulating energy, accessing emotions, effective for self-care, and is helpful for bereavement (McFerran, 2011). Telling stories and journaling not only keeps the connection to the deceased, but it brings comfort to the grieving. The Buffalo News (2015) shared quotes that were gathered by a mother, Mara Koven-Gelman and her friend Liz Pearl, from individuals who had lost a child, a parent, or a spouse, and used journaling as a method to maintain connections with their deceased loved ones; "Tell the story of death and you begin to acknowledge it. The love doesn't die when the person does. When people die, we inherit their stories" (The Buffalo News, 2015, p. 1).

As part of gaining understanding of the life altering experience of the death of a child, remaining connected through music, stories, art, journaling, and photographs is a precious and tender practice. For parents, acceptance that life as it was before the loss, will not return, changes the worldview, values, priorities, desires, identity, and sense of self.

CHAPTER 6: THE LIVED EXPERIENCE

The loss of a child is a phenomenon that changes the surviving parent. Autoethnography and ethnography offer a methodology in which the researcher can convey to the audience, deeply rich narratives of the personal experience, that may not be captured through other qualitative or quantitative methods. The purpose of this study was to examine the grief experience of a parent after the loss of a child. The study focused on the experience of the re-searcher and the participants, and attempted to validate the particulars of parent grief through ethnographic inquiry to generate an alternative grief model specific to the grief parents undergo after losing their children to death. Through reflective storytelling the horrendous and tender journey of grief as a parent, loss, identity, and personhood were explored. The loss of a child is a phenomenon that changes the surviving parent.

Restatement of the Purpose

Previous research and studies on parental grief and bereavement confirm the permanent alteration to a person's life, family, and identity (Barrera et al., 2007; Brotherson, 2000; Fletcher, 2002; Seecharan et al., 2004; Thomson, 2010). Through ethnographic inquiry, the study offers a thoughtful perspective with the purpose focused on (a) making known the individual parental experience of losing a child; (b) exploring the sociocultural factors of how a parent experiences loss; and (c) offer a framework of understanding the repercussions for therapists, psychologists, counselors, physicians, students, counselor educators, and parents.

Research Questions

Through an ethnographic methodology, the following research questions guided the study and help to gain deeper understanding and insight of the following:

Research question 1. What is the experience of

losing a child to death?

Research question 2. What sociocultural beliefs about death and grieving have been challenging throughout the grieving and acceptance process?

Research question 3. How has the personhood of the parent been changed since the death of their child?

Research Design

A qualitative research methodology with an ethnographic approach was used to focus on communicating the personal accounts of loss, grief, bereavement, and mourning. The ethnographic method was driven by the purpose of the study and the research questions, and provided the appropriate and necessary framework for the narrative. The researcher spent 11months reporting on her experience of loss after the death of her son. The data obtained from the researcher's journals and archives, were entered into the NVivo software program and coded. Themes were identified, and an overall context that contributes to an alternative grief model specific to parents was identified. The findings from the inquiry were synthesized with participant's responses to an open-ended questionnaire, to obtain feedback on their grief experience, and as a way to further validate the findings.

Ethnography

The ethnographic methodology includes a variety of types and procedures, with the main focus on gaining a deeper understanding of patterns, behaviors, and beliefs that a culture shares. Ethnographies, originated by anthropologists, can explore an entire culture of group, or a subset, or an individual, and the focus is on the behaviors of the people, not the culture (Creswell, 2013). Ethnography can include autoethnography, feminist ethnography, visual ethnography, confessional ethnography, realist ethnography, and critical ethnography, with the researcher often in the position of being an advocate. Critical ethnographers aim to empower people by opening up and highlighting the challenges of victimization, empowerment, challenging the status quo, and repression (Creswell). Specialized ethnographies focus more intently on a particular element or significant individual in the study (Fetterman, 2010). Fetterman (2010) shared that findings are often communicated through the addition of photographs, newspaper clippings, and recordings. The researcher could take an emic or an etic perspective. The emic perspective, as seen in this study, explores the perceptions of the insider, an approach that is crucial to understanding people's thoughts and behaviors. Focusing on a key individual allows the study to portray a richly detailed life history, while personal in nature and not completely reflective of an entire group, provides a picture of the group and one particular aspect (Fetterman, 2010). The ethnographer delves into some of the most sensitive and tender topics that people encounter, and the meanings that they create.

The task then is not to find the truth, but to uncover the meaning that people ascribe to life events, objects, activities, and other people (Ladner, 2016). The flexibility of ethnographic research takes the lived experience of the participants, and allows the data to evolve into a set of organized results (Creswell, 2013).

The data that was collected through the personal experience of the researcher was coded with the NVivo software program to first identify items that fit into the broad categories of biological and physical, psychological, and sociological responses.

Once the data was uploaded into the NVivo program, open coding was used among the narrative vignettes, the journals, photographs, and other artifacts to discover common thoughts, behaviors, feelings, practices, sociological influences, and physical responses to the loss of her son. During this step, the researcher, was looking for enough information to saturate each category (Creswell, 2014).

The physical responses were consistent with what the literature shared that also included increased crying, low energy, loss of appetite, stomach pain, tightness in the chest, and weight loss as being consistent with the parental response to losing a child to death. The psychological responses experienced were consistent with the psychological responses shared in the literature, and with the existing grief models. The sociological influences that appeared in the data related to societal and cultural practices were supported by the literature, and further, the literature explained the benefits of religion and spirituality as healing factors during grief, and beliefs about death and the cultural practices our society participates in to bring understanding and to honor the deceased, and the importance of maintaining connections with the deceased through storytelling, continuing with family traditions, and talking.

Working from the three major biopsychosocial categories, the data was examined using axial coding to make connections and identify the central phenomenon of the grief experience. Selective coding was the final step to uncover the story between all three categories (Creswell, 2014). A set of six specific themes began to emerge that not only described the experience and the story of loss, but also began to form a framework for a future grief model that is not confined by linearity, but shaped by the fluidity of the experience of grief.

The six themes identified were the importance of preserving the connection with the deceased, the importance of allowing time to understand and make meaning of the loss, the act of reworking a person's life to integrate and accommodate the grief rather than expect pre-life functioning to return, making an effort to reach out for support with friends, family, spirituality, finding strength in new and other behaviors, cultural practices, relationships to take on each new day, and taking time to allow oneself to naturally grieve the loss of the loved one, as well as taking time to care for oneself and to continue to live in the process. The themes are listed based on the frequency that they appeared in the data; however, there is no particular order to how a person might experience these themes.

The themes are placed in the acronym PARENT to help others remember the model as a reference tool. The themes do not indicate that one is more important than another, or has to occur in a linear way. The themes, consistent with the literature, represent a deeper and richer understanding of how grief shows up in the bereaved parent's life, identified and discovered by the frequency. Grief has a biological, a psychological, and a sociological nature that is circular. The data and the literature share that a person returns to many feelings, thoughts, and behaviors over and over again. The challenge and distinction of this study is to convey to the audience that grief is not a linear experience that must be bridled by steps. The themes merely represent the recurrent experiences that the researcher and participants share.

CHAPTER 7: A PARENT MODEL OF GRIEF

The experience of losing a child to death is ineffable. It is one that only another parent who undergoes this event can truly understand. The findings from this study indicate that the grief may change over time, may return to previous states again, is a unique experience, and is expected to remain for the parent's lifetime. What this means is that grief is not an illness, not a mental disorder, but is the natural response to losing a loved one. While a grief model could be helpful in understanding grief, normalizing the many thoughts and feelings that accompany grief, and provide an example of what to expect, the grief model must be appropriate to the type of grief and allow for circularity and fluidity in the grief. The themes of the PARENT Model of Grief are as follows.

Theme 1: preserving connections. The importance of *preserving* the connection and bond with the deceased is explained in Bowlby's theory of grief that identifies that even in death the attachment bonds between a parent and a child, the psychological response to comfort, protect, and provide safety, do not end (Thomson, 2010). Neimeyer, Klass, and Dennis (2014) have done extensive research to support that part of learning to live with loss, adjusting one's worldview, and making meaning, occur with a realignment of the relations with the deceased to continue with the bonds of attachment even with the physical absence. After death communications, odors, symbolic phenomena, prayer, meditation, visitation dreams, spirituality, visions, physical sensations, and premonitions experienced by parents after the death of their children improved their psychological health (Ganzevoort & Falkenburg, 2012; Sormanti & August, 1997). Sormanti and August (1997), and Walsh and colleagues (2002), shared that the best way to manage grief is to integrate the death event and the deceased into life. After death communications are considered normal reactions to grief and are not considered to be pathological (Kwilecky, 2011; Sormanti & August, 1997). Preserving the connection and the bonds with the deceased is a healthy coping response that tends to the attachment bonds, helps the parent maintain his or her identity, and is helpful in adjusting to the loss (Sormanti & August, 1997; Steffen & Coyle, 2010). Storytelling, journaling, photographs, videos, and recalling favorite songs are additional ways for parents to continue to create connections, and bring comfort to the grieving process. The data shared that these continued connections provided the researcher and participants with hope and small answers in times of distress, confusion, and fear, and nurtured the attachment bond that still remained.

Theme 2: allow time. *Allow* time to experience all the important, significant, and complex feelings, thoughts, experiences, and behaviors that accompany grief and loss without a time limit. Recovery is not the goal for successful grieving (Thomson, 2010). To lose a child to death is the most profoundly distressing and painful journey that a human being will every undergo. The loss effects all facets of life (Barrera et al., 2007) and alters the family and individual permanently. As a response, parents often are consumed with guilt that they failed in protecting their child, that they did not respond appropriately prior to death, during, or after, and that it is their fault or somehow the death is a punishment for their own wrongdoings (Bryant, 2003). Parents experience hopelessness, anger, disbelief, confusion, and regret at the loss of their future, their lineage, their child's future, the incongruent premature separation, and pain that they will not see their child age. When parents lose a child to a violent sudden death, additional psychological complications occur at a more intense level (Lohan & Murphy, 2007; Worden, 2008). The data revealed that at times screaming, crying, being with the many desperate thoughts, feelings, and behaviors were all part of the experience and necessary for the parent to begin to adjust to the immense loss of their child. A bereaved person could feel less distress if he or she allows for natural healing to take place, without expectations or judgments from self or others to experience grief in stages. Biopsychosocial responses shift and change, and do not often occur in a linear manner.

Theme 3: rework life. *Rework* the story of life includes grief and learning to live with the loss versus acceptance. Pre-loss functioning is not the goal, rather, grief is adapted into a very dissimilar life that includes the loss of the child (Thomson, 2010). The acceptance piece is only that life is not as it was before the loss, and that the child, nor that time, will return, which alters the parent's sense of self, identity, values, worldview, priorities, and desires. Removing the pressure to resolve grief in a linear timeframe, provides more fluidity to move from many feelings and responses as needed. The data exposed a continual cycle of feeling many different emotions and cognitions, sometimes all in the same moment, and how the parents attempted to integrate these feelings and thoughts into their current level of functioning, rather than to attempt to regain what once was. Fear, sickness, distress, worry, pain, confusion, shock, and low energy and many other responses were identified as happening all at once or over different periods of time. The data shared that while attempting to overcome these thoughts and feelings is often not possible, integrating these facets of grief into life, a person is more able to achieve a different level of understanding without pressure to return to how life once was.

Theme 4: effort to reach out. Make an *effort* to reach out when able to let others help in carrying the immense weight of the grief. Families are going through the loss together and are often helpful in distributing the experience of grief. Parental grief and grief that surviving grandparents and siblings are experiencing puts about 19% of the population in the position of suffering and dealing with loss (Seecharan et al., 2004). At times parents might rather isolate, and that is absolutely appropriate. Still, the data indicated that when the researcher had support in the grief, the grief felt lighter. Professionals such as therapists, psychologists, and counselors are also effective resources to help understand and adjust to the loss. They may have been through their own loss, they have supported others who have experienced a similar loss, or they could just offer a safe place to cry, talk, grieve, scream, express, and experience all the various emotions, thoughts, and behaviors that accompany the immense grief of losing a child to death. A friend or family member might be appointed to handle the logistics of after death tasks so parents are not completely overwhelmed.

Theme 5: new reason. Find a *new* reason to get up each morning and realize that every day will be accompanied with new feelings, thoughts, and behaviors, and that is okay. The data shared that prayer and spiritual beliefs were helpful for the parents in getting up out of bed in the morning, taking on each day, being able to continue. In addition, parents found strength from focusing on particular phrases of empowerment, prayer, affirmations and finding purpose and strength in the role of a parent for surviving children, or as a loved one with other family members. Strobe and Schut's (as cited in Smit, 2015) Dual Process Model also indicated a need to adjust to new routines and the external changes to life. At times parents have to find a new reason to get through the next five minutes of their life. The data shared it is important to have a purpose each day that is motivating enough to tackle the day or moment, even in the throughs of grief.

Theme 6: take breaks. *Take breaks* from life to be able to grieve the loved one, as well as take breaks or allow distraction from grief to be able to live. Consistent with the Stroebe and Schut's (as cited in Smit, 2015) Dual Process model, taking breaks from grief is an adaptive tool. Because of the significant distress that occurs after losing a child to death, distracting from the sorrow and anguish is necessary to survival. In addition, as grief shifts, the data indicated the importance of taking breaks from grief to live. This can be difficult and produce guilt in the beginning, but as the parent reworks the loss into current life, the breaks will be vital to biological and psychological health. The data shared that parents felt guilty at times or confused if they were not overcome with grief, and some felt more connected to their child when fully grieving. The literature supports that it is healthy and necessary to allow a person time to not only grieve and connect but to take time away from grief for psychological strength and wellbeing.

Whereas the existing grief models are harmonious with the data in some ways, they lack the fluidity and the circularity that was noticed in the data. The Kubler-Ross model suggested a linear process of visiting particular stages on the route to acceptance, however, the data showed a continual movement between many different feelings and thoughts around grief, often recycling over and over between the thoughts of disbelief, sadness, and sorrow. These six facets integrate into the central theme of a specific grief model, the PARENT Model of Grief developed by the researcher, that addresses the complexities and unique needs of parents who have lost a child to death.

A PARENT Model of Grief Condensed

P*reserve Connections*. Talking to the deceased, sharing stories, listening to the deceased's favorite music, journaling, dreaming, spiritual visitations, looking at photographs, drawing, watching videos, meditation, and visiting the grave site are all ways to continue the connection, keep the attachment bonds between parent and child nurtured, and are normal responses to loss. Recognizing for yourself when it is time to let go, or to maintain the bond, and that both are okay.

Allow Time. Give yourself time to feel and think everything you need to feel and think, and time to distract. Allow time to cry, to scream, to hide, to sleep, to yearn, and to adjust to the loneliness. Do not have a timeline on grief. Because of the incongruency of losing a child to death, grieving is often a lifelong event. It will change in its presentation and move in different directions. Grief is not a process. It is an overwhelming shift in life, beliefs, worldview, and your personhood. There is no right or wrong way to grieve.

Rework Life. Life after child loss will be different. Your role and identity have changed as a result of the loss. Life is not the same, and you are not the same. Integration and assimilation of grief and loss will take time. The only aspect of *acceptance* that applies to parental grief is accepting and understanding that the goal is not to return to pre-loss functioning.

Effort. Make an effort to reach out to loved ones, support systems, spiritual support systems, God, therapists, counselors, psychologists, family, and friends. Let others help carry the overwhelming load of grief and understand that at times reaching out will also be difficult to do. Make an effort, do not force yourself. At times people will say things that are stupid and of no help. Take your time and know that others are there to listen.

*N*ew. Everyday find a new reason to keep going, a new prayer to say, a new motivational statement, a new reason to get out of bed in the morning, a new emotion to feel, a new thought, a new behavior, a new memory, a new spiritual experience, a new fear, a new response. Remind yourself that it is okay to feel the scary things, and the pleasant things.

*T*ake Breaks. The experience of grief is biologically, psychologically, and sociologically draining and painful. It often comes in waves. Allow yourself to take breaks from life to grieve. Allow yourself to take breaks from grief to live. Develop your own mental life preserver to grab when the waves hit.

Life has forever changed, we have forever changed, and it should be that way. Our children were so special to us, no matter their age. We are parents who have lost our greatest joys. For some of us, we have surviving children who we still love and care for. That does not take away that one of our children is no longer with us. Although many of us believe we know where our children's souls have gone, or what death means to us, even if we believe we will see them again, we miss them now. We yearn for them now. And that will not change. What this means for this study is that it is okay to change after losing a child, and it is perhaps unavoidable. There is not a right or a wrong way to grieve, which has been stated often in the field of grief work, yet, at times the bereaved are still shunned. They are expected to grieve for a time period. Individuals, caregivers, those in the helping field, counselors, therapists, and physicians can be very helpful with the bereaved by recognizing the tremendous impact of losing a child to death, and convey this understanding to those who are grieving. In a place where nothing makes sense after losing a child, it could be very helpful to at least know that your grieving does not have to make sense or follow an order either.

The PARENT model understands and embraces the attachment patterns between child and parent, the profound alteration to life that occurs after a child's death, and the circular nature of grief and bereavement. The model differs from current grief models in that it recognizes that each person's grief experience is unique, circular, supports research in that the loss of a child is a devastating and lifelong event, and removes the judgment and pressure to accept and recover. The PARENT Grief Model, developed by the researcher who is also a grieving parent, is a framework to help parents feel supported, understood, and normal in their grief, touching upon the main facets that parents struggle with starting from the moment they learn that they have lost their child to death.

EPILOGUE

The autoethnographic and ethnographic methodology was valuable in studying the experience of loss and grief on the personhood of a mother and a psychotherapist. I have seen shifts in my grief, and I continue to see that happen. I have learned that I cannot run away from the pain, but it is necessary to take breaks. This journey will be on going, and will definitely continue to change. Everyone will navigate grief differently. It is important that individuals find their own way through loss. There is not a right or wrong way to deal with grief and loss, and feelings, thoughts, and behaviors will manifest in unique ways.

I continue to grieve my son, but I am finding that I can work, teach, consult, parent, write, and live with the grief better now than in the beginning. I weep for myself and for my family, as I complete this book. This event has not been easy, and I do not expect it to get easier. My son's life, as I have described, was valuable and precious. There is no one like him, and there will never be. I know I will grieve him to the end of my own life. I would just like to learn how to live with the pain, and I think I am doing that. Grief takes time. We will all lose loved ones, and we too will be lost. I am thankful for the strength God gives me each day. I will continue my spiritual journey, strengthening my faith, and I hope my experience with loss is of value to my work as a therapist, my being as a human, and my soul.

The PARENT Model of Grief understands and embraces the attachment patterns between child and parent, the profound alteration to life that occurs after a child's death, and the circular nature of grief and bereavement. The model differs from current grief models in that it recognizes that each person's grief experience is unique, supports research in that the loss of a child is a devastating and lifelong event, and removes the judgment and pressure to accept and recover. The PARENT Grief Model is a framework to help parents feel supported, understood, and normal in their grief, touching upon the main facets that parents struggle with starting from the moment they learn that they have lost their child to death. The grief experience keeps the parents connected to their children. Grief is an outlet for pain, a method of turning inward, a way to understand and process. Grief does not seem to follow a linear set of stages, nor does it appear to be a process. Grief is unique to every being. Grief is not a mental disorder, nor an illness. It is the natural response to losing someone with whom you were attached. It comes and it goes, it changes over time, and sometimes returns back to where it started.

This study provides implications for parents, researchers, clinicians, physicians, psychotherapists, psychologists, friends, family, and others who live long enough to lose someone they love, or help others who have. By acknowledging and understanding the unique nuances of parent grief, those who are experiencing it or those who are treating those who are experiencing it, can have an alternative model of grief that is based on the actual needs of grieving parents.

Secondly, an implication for practice is for educators in the helping field, to take into account the uniqueness of parent guilt, the significant needs that parents have after losing their child to death, and to be mindful that many parents do not believe they will recover from grief. They believe that grief will be a lifelong event. Acceptance is not the goal. Living with the grief, adapting to life again with the grief, and learning a new normal are the steps parents are taking to continue with life in their grief. Educators and clinicians must take into consideration that bereavement and grieving are not pathological in themselves. Additional complications can arise that can further be aggravated by grief, such as biological and physical responses like illness, cancer, and loss of energy, and psychological response such as depression, isolation, and suicidal thoughts. I also believe that the PARENT Grief Model offers a different approach to grief that normalizes the experience that parents undergo after the loss of their children. This model could benefit students, clinicians, and other parents who are trying to make sense of their own grief.

"I love when people that have been through hell walk out of the flames carrying buckets of water for those still consumed by the fire"-Stephanie Sparkles.

ABOUT THE AUTHOR

Dr. Tracy S. Kelly

Dr. Tracy Kelly is a psychotherapist, an adjunct professor, a consultant, and a writer/researcher. After the death of her son in 2015, Dr. Kelly researched the grief experience after child loss and developed a framework specific to this type of bereavement.

REFERENCES

Abelman, R., & Neuendorf, K. (1987). Themes and topics
   in religious television programming. Review
   of Religious Research, 29(2), 152-74. Retrieved
   from http://www.jstor.org/stable/3511724

Adams, T. E., Jones, S. H., & Ellis, C.
   (2015). Autoethnography: Understanding
   qualitative research. New York, NY: Oxford
   University Press.

American Psychiatric Association. (2013). *Diagnostic
   and statistical manual of mental disorders:*
   DMS-5. Washington, DC: American Psychiatric
   Association.

Amplified Bible (2015). The Lockman Foundation, La
   Habra, CA.

Ainsworth, T. (2011). *Exploring the process of grief
   experienced by a parent following the death of a*

child (Order No. 3485957). Available from ProQuest Central; ProQuest Dissertations & Theses Global. (909056848). Retrieved from http://search.proquest.com/ docview/909056848?accountid=34899

Aponte, H. J., Powell, F. D., Brooks, S., Watson, M. F., Litzke, C., Lawless, J., & Johnson, E. (2009). Training the person of the therapist in an academic setting. *Journal of Marital and Family Therapy, 35*(4), 381-394. doi: 101111/ j.1752- 0606.2009.00123.x

Arnold, J., & Buschman Gemma, P. (2008). The continuing process of parental grief.*Death Studies, 32*(7), 658-673. Doi:10.1080/07481180802215718

Arnold, J., Gemma, P., & Cushman, L. (2005). Exploring parental grief: Combining quantitative and qualitative measures. *Archives of Psychiatric Nursling, 19*(6), 245-255. doi:10.1016/j.apnu.2005.07.008

Babylonian Talmud. Isidore Ebstein.(Ed.). London England: Soncino P. 1990. Baldock, J. (2013). *The Tibetan book of the dead.* London, England, Arcturus.

Barrera, M., D'Agostino, N., Schneiderman, G., Tallett, S., Spencer, L., & Jovcevska, V. (2007). Patterns of parental bereavement following the loss of a child and related factors. *Omega: Journal of Death & Dying, 55*(2), 145-167, doi:10.2190/ OM.55.2.d

Bauman, Z. (2005). *Liquid life.* Cambridge, UK: Polity Press.

Becker, E. (1973). *The denial of death.* New York, NY: Free Press.

Benziman, G., Kannai, R., & Ahmad, A. (2012). The wounded healer as cultural archetype. *CLCWeb: Comparative Literature and Culture, 14*(1); http:// dx.doi.org/10.7771/1481-4374.19 27

Bergmann, M. S. (2011). The dual impact of Freud's death and Freud's death instinct theory on the history of psychoanalysis. *Psychoanalytic Review, 98*(5), 665-86. doi:http:// dx.doi.org/101521prev2011986665

Bernard, H. R., & Ryan, G. W. (2010). *Analyzing qualitative data. Systematic approaches.* SAGE. Thousand Oaks, CA.

Beyond the five stages of grief. (2011). *Harvard Mental Health Letter, 28*(6), 3-3.
Retrieved from EBSCOhost Database.

Blair, J. (2003). Bearing the worst news, then helping the
healing. New York Times.
Retrieved from https://login.libproxy.edmc.edu/login? url=http://search.proquest.com/docview/432334554? accountid=34899

Bochner, A. P. (2002). Perspective on inquiry III: The moral of stories. In Mark L. Knapp & John A. Dlay (Eds.), *Handbook of interpersonal communication* (3rd ed).
p. 73-101. Thousand Oaks, CA: SAGE

Bochner, A. P., & Ellis, C. (2002). *Ethnographically speaking: Autoethnography, literature, and aesthetics.* Walnut Creek, CA: AltaMira Press.

Bochner, A. P., & Ellis, C. (2016). *Evocative autoethnography; Writing lives and telling stories.* New York: Taylor & Francis

Bogensperger, J., & Leuger-Schuster, B. (2014). Losing a child: Finding meaning in bereavement.

European Journal of Psychotraumatology, 5. doi http://dx.doi.org/10.3402/ejpt.v5.22910

Bowlby, J. (1980). *Loss: Sadness and depression* (Vol. 3). New York, NY: Penguin Books.

Bowlby, J. (1988). A secure base: *Parent-child attachment and healthy human development.* New York, NY: Basic Books.

Brent, C. (1998). Favourite prayers: The ship. *British Medical Journal, 317*(7174), 1727. Retrieved from ProQuest Database May 27, 2016.

Broadbent, J. (2013). The bereaved therapist speaks. An interpretative phenomenological analysis of humanistic therapists' experiences of a significant personal bereavement and its impact upon their therapeutic practice: An exploratory study. *Counselling & Psychotherapy Research, 13*(4), 263-271, 9p. Retrieved from Ebscohost database.

Brotherson, S. E. (2000). Parental accounts of a child's death: Influences on parental identity and behavior (Order No. 9961-1446). Available from ProQuest Dissertations & Theses Global.

(304613995). Retrieved from http:// serach.proquest.com/docview/304613995? accountid=34899

Bryant, C. D. (2003). *Handbook of death & dying.* Thousand Oaks, CA: SAGE. Buglass, E. (2010). Grief and bereavement theories. *Nursing Standard, 24*(41), 44-47. Retrieved from http://www.journals.rcni.com

Burge, D. (2015, June). Cavalry scouts' job is same since wild west days. *Corpus Christi Caller-Times* Retrieved from https://login.libproxy.edmc.edu/login? url=http://search.proquest.com/docview/16 91773264?accountid=34899

Callahan, J. L., & Dittloff, M. (2007). Through a glass darkly: Reflections on therapist transformations. *Professional Psychology: Research and Practice, 38*(6), 547- 553. doi:http:// dx.doi.org.libproxy.edmc.edu/10.1037/073 5-7028.38.6.547

Chang, H. (2008). *Auto-ethnography as method.* Walnut Creek, CA: Left Coast Press. Collins, E.

(n.d.). *Grief that never dies: Gold star mothers share their stories*. Soldiers:

The official U.S. Army Magazine. Retrieved from http://www.soldiers.dodlive.mil

Conchar, C., & Repper, J. (2014). "Walking wounded or wounded healer?" does personal experience of mental health problems help or hinder mental health practice? A review of the literature. *Mental Health and Social Inclusion, 18*(1), 35-44. doi:http://dx.doi.org/10.1108/ MHSI-02-2014-0003.

Cooperstein, M. A. (1992). The myths of healing: a summary of research into transpersonal healing experience. *Journal of Religion & Psychical research, 15*(2), 63. Retrieved from Ebscohost database May 19, 2016.

Creswell, J. W. (2013). *Qualitative inquiry and research design: Choosing among five approaches.* (3rd. ed.) Thousand Oaks, CA: SAGE.

Creswell, J. W. (2014). Research, design*: Qualitative, quantitative, and mixed methods approaches.* (4th ed.). Thousand Oaks, CA:

SAGE.

Davis-Konigsberg, R. (2011). *The truth about grief: The myth of its five stages and the new science of loss.* New York, NY: Simon and Schuster

Davies, R., (2004). New understanding of parental grief; Literature review. *Journal ofAdvanced Nursing, 46*(5), 506-513. doi:10.1111/ j.1365-2648.2004.03024.x

Dechesne, M., van den Berg, C., & Soeters, J. (2007). International collaboration underthreat: A field study in Kabul. Conflict Management and Peace Science, 24(1), 25-36. doi:10.1080/07388940601102811

Denney, J., & He, M. (2014). The social side of accidental death. *Social Science Research, 43*, 92-107. doi:10.1016/ j.ssresearch.2013.09.004

Dent, A. (2005). Supporting the bereaved: Theory and practice. *Counselling at Work, 15*, 22-23. Retrieved from http:// www.bacpworkplace.org.uk/journal_pdf/acw/ autumn05_ann.pdf

Doloriert, C., & Sambrook, S. (2009). Ethical confessions of the "I" of autoethnography: The student's dilemma. *Qualitative Research in Organizations and Management, 4*(1), 27-45. doi:http:// dx.doi.org/10.1108/17465640910951435

Drenth, C. N., Herbst, A. G., & Strydom, H. (2010). A complicated grief intervention model. *Health S A, 15*(1), 8-1A, 2A, 3A, 4A, 5A, 6A, 7A, 8A. Retrieved from https://login.libproxy.edmc.edu/login? url=http://serach.proquest.com/docview/74 8839357?accountid=34899

Egnew, T. R. (2005). The meaning of healing: transcending suffering. *Annals of Family Medicine, 3*(3), 255-262. doi:10.1370/afm.313

Elder, P. (1998). "Portrait of Family Grief," in *Loss and Bereavement: Managing Change,* edited by Ros Weston, Teryy Maring, and Yvonne Anderson. Oxford, UK: Blackwell Science.

Ellis, C. (2004). *The ethnographic I; A methodological novel about autoethnography.* Walnut Creek, CA: Alta Mira Press.

Ellis, C., & Bochner, A. P. (2000). Autoethnography, personal narrative, reflexivity. In Norman K. Denzin & Yvonna S. Lincoln (Eds.), *Handbook of qualitative research* (2nd ed., p. 733-768). Thousand Oaks, CA: SAGE

Ellis, C., Adams, T., & Bochner, A. (2011). Autoethnography: An overview. *Qualitative Social Research, 12*(1) Retrieved from http://search.proquest.com/docview/870465772?accountid=34899

Ellis, C., & Ellingson, L. (2000). Qualitative methods. In Edgar Borgatta & Rhonda Montgomery (Eds.), Encyclopedia of sociology (p. 2287-2296). New York, NY: Macmillan.

Ellingson, L. (2009). Engaging crystallization in qualitative research, An introduction. SAGE Publications, Inc.

Euripides. (1958). The suppliant women. In D. Grene, & R. Lattimore (Eds.), *Euripides IV* (pp. 51-105). Chicago, IL: University of Chicago Press. (Original work published 423 bc).

Evison, M. (2012). *Death of a soldier: A mother's story*. London, England: Biteback. Faust, D. G.

(2008). *This republic of suffering: Death and the American Civil War.* New York, NY: Alfred A. Knopf.

Fetterman, D. M. (2010). *Ethnography. Step-by-step.* (3rd ed.). Thousand Oaks, CA: SAGE.

Field, M., & Behrman. (2003). *When children die: Improving palliate and end-of-life care for children and their families.* Washington, DC: National Academies Press. ProQuest ebrary.

Field, N. (2008). Whether to relinquish or maintain a bond with the deceased. M. H. Stroebe, R. O. Schut, H. & Stroebe, W. *Handbook of bereavement research and practice; advances in theory and intervention.* Washington, American Psychological Association Press.

Finding hope: Casualty assistance officers help grieving families. (2010). *US Fed News Service, Including US State News.* Retrieved from https://login.libproxy.edmc.edu/login?url=http://search.proquest.com/docview/759765454?accountid=34899

Fletcher, P. (2002). Experiences in family

bereavement. *Family & Community Health,* *25*(1), 57-70. Retrieved from Ebscohost Database.

Garner, B. A., & Black, H. C. (1999). *Black's law dictionary.* St. Paul, MN: West Group.

Ganzevoort, R. R., & Falkenburg, N. (2012). Stories beyond life and death: Spiritual experiences of continuity and discontinuity among parents who lose a child. *Journal of Empircal Theology, 25*(2), 189-204. doi:10.1163/15709256-12341249

Georgescu, M. (2011). The duality between life and death instincts in Freud.

Contemporary Readings in Law and Social Justice, 3(1), 134-139. Retrieved from https://login.libproxy.edmc.edu/login?url=http://search.proquest.com/docview/897101448?acountid=34899

Gibbs, D., Rae Olmsted, K., Brown, J., & Clinton-Sherrod, A. (2011). Dynamics of stigma for alcohol and mental health treatment among army soldiers. *Military Psychology, 23*(1), 36-51. DOI: 10.1080/08995605.2011.534409

Hall, C. (2011). Beyond Kübler-Ross: Recent developments in our understanding of grief and bereavement. *InPsych, 33*(6), 8-11. Retrieved from https://www.psychology.org.au

Hamama-Raz, Y., Rosenfeld, S., & Buchbinder, E. (2010). Giving birth to life-again! Bereaved parents' experiences with children born following the death of an adult son. *Death Studies, 34*(5), 381-403. doi:10.1080/07481181003697613

Hastings, S. O., Musambira, G. W., & Hoover, J. D. (2007). Community as a key to healing after the death of a child. *Communication & Medicine (De Gruyter), 4*(2), 153-163. doi:10.1515/CAM.2007.019

Hasui, C., & Kitamura, T. (2004). Aggression and guilt during mourning by parents who lost an infant. *Bulletin of the Menninger Clinic, 68*(3) 245-259. doi:http://dx.doi.org/abs101521bumc68324540403

Heim, C. (2012). Tutorial facilitation in the humanities based on the tenets of Carl Rogers.

Higher Education (00181560), 63(3), 289-298. doi:10.1007/s10734-011- 9441-z

Hendrickson, K. (2009). Morbidity, mortality, and parental grief: A review of the literature on the relationship between the death of a child and the subsequent health of parents. *Palliative & Supportive Care, 7*(1), 109-19. doi:http://dx.doi.org/10.1017/ S1478951509000133

Hennink, M. M., Hutter, I., & Bailey, A. (2011). *Qualitative research methods.* London: SAGE.

Hensley, P. L., & Clayton, P. J. (2008). Bereavement: Signs, symptoms, and course. *Psychiatric Annals, 38*(10), 649-654. Retrieved from https://login.libproxy.edmc.edu/login? url=http://search.proquest.com/ docview/217057180?accountid=34899

Housman, A. E. (1983). The an athlete dying young. The Norton Anthology of Poetry (3rd ed.) Retrieved from http://www. http:// www.poetryfoundation.org/poems- and- poets/poems/detail/46452

Jones, E. (2011). Alcohol use and misuse within

the military: A review. *International Review of Psychiatry, 23*(2), 166-172. Retrieved from EBSCO database.

Jung, C. G. (1979), "Fundamental questions of psychotherapy", in Read, H., Fordham, M., Adler, G., & McGuire, W. (Eds), *The collected works of C. G. Jung* (Vol. 16), Princeton University Press, Princeton, NJ, 116-25.

Jung, C. G., Shamdasani, S., Kyburz, M., Peck, J., & Hoerni,
U. (n.d.).*The red book =Liber novus.*

Kahn, S., & Liefooghe, A. (2014). Thanatos: Freudian manifestations of death at work. *Culture & Organization, 20*(1), 53-67. doi:10.1080/14759551.2013.853064

Kaplow, J., Layne, C., Saltzman, W., Cozza, S., & Pynoos, R. (2013). Using multidimensional grief theory to explore the effects of deployment, reintegration, and death on military youth and families. *Clinical Child and Family Psychology Review, 16*(3), 322-40. doi:http://dx.doi.org/10.1007/s10567-013-0143-1

Kenny, G. (2012, February). The healers journey: A literature review. *Complementary Therapies in Clinical Practice, 18*(1), 31-36. doi:10.1016/j.ctcp.2011.09.002

Kouriatis, K., & Brown, D. (2013). Therapists' experience of loss: an interpretative phenomenological analysis. *Omega – The Journal of Death and Dying (Farmindale), 89*(2). doi:10.2190/OM.68.2.a

Kristensen, P., Heir, T., Herlofsen, P., Langsrud, A., & Weisaeth, L. (2012). Parental mental health after the accidental death of a son during military service: 23 year follow-up study. *Journal of Nervous and Mental Disease, 200,* 63-68. doi:10.1097/NMD.0b013e31823e5796

Kristensen, P., Weisaeth, L., & Heir, T. (2012). Bereavement and mental health after sudden and violent losses: A review. *Psychiatry, 75*(1), 76-97. doi:http://dx.doi.org/101521psych201275176

Kung, H., Hoyert, D., Xu, J., & Murphy, S. (2005). National Vital Statistics Reports. Center for

Disease Control. Retrieved from cdc.gov

Kwilecki, S. (2011). Ghosts, meaning, and faith: After-death communications in bereavement narratives. *Death Studies, 35*(3), 219-243. doi:10.1080/07481187.2010.511424

Ladner, S. (2016). *Practical ethnography: A guide to doing ethnography in the private sector.* Walnut Creek, US: Routledge. Retrieved from http://www.ebrary.com.libproxy.edmc.edu

La Pointe, K. (2010). Narrating career, positioning identity: Career identity as a narrative practice. *Journal of Vocational Behavior, 77*(1), 1-9. doi:10.1016/j.jvb.2010.04.003

Lebenswelt (Life-World). (2011). In B. Sandywell, *Dictionary of visual discourse: A dialectical lexicon of terms.* Surrey, United Kingdom: Ashgate Publishing. Retrieved from http://libproxy.edmc.edu/login?url=http://literati,credoreference.com/content/entr y/ashgtvd/lebenswelt_life_workd/0

Leedy, P. D., & Ormrod, J. E. (2009). *Practical research: Planning and design* (9th ed.). Upper Saddle River, NJ: Prentice Hall.

Leong, F. T. (2008). Encyclopedia of counseling. Thousand Oaks, CA: SAGE. Lester, D. (2015). Self-construal and the fear of death. *Psychological Reports, 117*(2), 376-379. doi:10.2466/16.PRO.117C23z0

Lewandowski-Romps, L., Peterson, C., Berglund, P., Collins, S., Cox, K., Hauret, K., . . . Herringa, S. (2014). Risk factors for accident death in the U.S. Army, 2004-2009. *American Journal of Preventative Medicine, 47*(6), 745-753. doi.org/10.1016/j.amepre.2014.07.052

Lewis, C. S. (2001). A grief observed. San Francisco: Harper San Francisco Lohan, J. A., & Murphy, S. A. (2007). Bereaved mothers' marital status and family functioning after a child's sudden, violent death: A preliminary study. *Journal of Loss & Trauma, 112*(4), 333-347. Retrieved from EBSCOhost Database.

Longfellow, H. W. (1866, April). Killed at the ford. *The Atlantic.* Retrieved from www.theatlantic.com

Lutz, T. (1999). *Crying: The natural and cultural*

history of tears. New York, NY: W. W. Norton.

Malkinson, R., Rubin, S. S., & Witztum, E. (2006). Therapeutic issues and the relationship to the deceased: Working clinically with the two-track model of bereavement. *Death Studies, 30*(9), 797-815. doi:10.1080/07481180600884723

Mancha, B., Watkins, E., Nichols, J., Seguin, P., & Bell, A. (2014). Mortality surveillance in the U.S. army 2005-2011. *Military Medicine, 179*(12), 1478-86. Retrieved from http://search.proquest.com/docview/1636191409?accountid=34899

Mannino, J. D. (1997). *Grieving days, healing days.* Boston, MA: Allyn & Bacon. May, R. (1983). *The discovery of being: Writing in existential psychology.* New York, NY Norton.McFerran, K. (2011). Music therapy with bereaved youth: Expressing grief and feeling better. *Prevention Researcher, 18*(3), 17-20. Retrieved from EBSOhost Database.

Mendez, M. (2013). Autoethnography as a research method: Advantages, limitations and criticisms. *Columbian Applied Linguistics*

Journal, 15(2), 279-287. Retrieved from EBSCO Host Database.

Miller, L. (2008). Death notification for families of homicide victims: Healing dimensions of a complex process. *Omega: Journal of Death & Dying, 57*(4), 367-380. doi:10.2190/OM.57.4.c

Miro. (2014). Fortitude. *Warrior Poet Wisdom.* Retrieved from http://warriorpoetwisdom.com/2014/03/09/fortitude/#comments

Molitor, F., & Sapolsky, B. S. (1993). Sex, violence, and victimization in slasher films. *Journal of Broadcasting and Electronic Media, 37*(2), 233-242. doi:10.1080/08838159309364218

Nabben, J. (2014). The science behind storytelling. Washington, DC: Melcrum Smarter Internal Communication. Retrieved from https://www.melcrum.com/research/strategy-planning-tactics/science-behing-storytelling. Retrieved June 10, 2016

Niño, A., Kissil, K., & Apolinar Claudio, F. L. (2015).

Perceived professional gains of master's level students following a person-of-the-therapist training program: A retrospective content analysis. *Journal of Marital and Family Therapy, 41*(2), 16

Oppy, G., & Trakakis, N. N. (2014). *Twentieth-century philosophy of religion*. Durham, GB: Routledge. ProQuest ebrary. Retrieved, may 22, 2016.

Opler, M. E. (1945). Themes as dynamic forces in culture. *American Journal of Sociology, 51,* 198-206.

Ott, C., Lueger, R., Kelber, T., & Prigerson, H. (2007). Spousal bereavement in older adults: Common, resilient, and chronic grief with defining characteristics. *Journal of Nervous & Mental Disease, 195*(4), 332-341. Retrieved at mcbi.nlm.nig.gov

Palmquist, S. R. (2011). *Cultivating personhood: Kant and Asian philosophy*. Berlin/Boston, DE: De Gruyter. ProQuest ebrary. Retrieved May 6, 2016

Parkes, C. M., & Weiss, R. (1983). *Recovery from*

bereavement. New York, NY: Basic Books.

Peck, D. L., & Bryant, C. D. (2009). *Encyclopedia of Death and the Human Experience.* Thousand Oaks, CA: SAGE Publications, Inc. Retrieved from EBSCOhost Database.

Raphael, B. (1994). *The anatomy of bereavement.* New York, NY: Basic Books. Rinopoche, S., Gaffney, P., & Harvey, A. (1992). *The Tibetan book of living and dying.* San Francisco, CA: Harper San Francisco.

Rogers, C. R. (1980). *A way of being.* Boston, MA: Houghton Mifflin.

Rogers, C. R. (1995). *On becoming a person: A therapist's view of psychotherapy.* Boston, MA: Houghton, Mifflin.

Rogers, C., Floyd, F., Seltzer, M., Greenberg, J., & Hong, J. (2008). Long-term effects of the death of a child on parents' adjustment in midlife. *Journal of Family Psychology, 22,* 203-211. doi: http:// dx.doi.org/10.1037/0893-3200.22.2.203

Roos, S. (2012). The Kubler-Ross model: An esteemed relic. *Gestalt Review,*

16(3), 312-315. Retrieved from Ebscohost database.

Rossman, G. B., & Rallis, S. F. (2003). Learning in the field: An introduction to qualitative research (2nd ed.). Thousand Oaks, CA: SAGE.

Rubin, S., & Malkinson, R. (2001). Parental response to child loss across the life cycle: Clinical and research perspective. In M. S. Stroebe, R. O. Hansson, W. Stroebe, & H. Schut (Eds.), Handbook of bereavement research: Consequences, coping and care (pp. 219-240). Washington, DC: American Psychological Association.

Sage Publications, & Leong, F. L. (2008). *Encyclopedia of counseling*. Los Angeles, CA: SAGE.

Salakari, A., Kaunonen, M., & Aho, A. L. (2014). Negative changes in a couple's relationship after a child's death. *Interpersonal, 8*(2), 193-209. Retrieved from https://login.libproxy.edmc.edu/login?url=http://search.proquest.com/docview/1682033515?accountid=34899

Schecter, H,. & Everitt, D. (1997). *The A-Z encyclopedia of serial killers.* New York, NY: Pocket Books.

Schultz, R. (1979). Death anxiety: Intuitive and empirical perspectives. Pp. 66-87 in *Death and Dying: Theory/Research/Practice,* edited by Larry A. Busen. Dubuque, IA: William C. Brown.

Seecharan, G., Andresen, E., Norris, K., & Toce, S. (2004). Parents' assessment of quality of care and grief following a child's death. *Archives of Pediatrics & Adolescent Medicine, 158(6),* 515-520. doi:10.1001/archpedi.158.6.515.

Shepard, J. J. (2005). Helping grieving people: When tears are not enough: A handbook for care providers. Florence, KY: Brunner-Routledge. ProQuest ebrary.

Singer, J. A. (2004). Narrative identity and meaning making across the adult lifespan: An introduction. *Journal of Personality, 72(3),* 437-460. doi:10.111/

j.0022/3506.2004.00268x

Smit, C. (2015). Theories and models of grief: Applications to professional practice. *Whitireia Nursing & Health journal, (22)*, 33-37. Retrieved from https:// login.libproxy.edmc.edu/login? url=http:// serach.proquest.com/docview/1764369528? accountid=34899

Soeters, J. L., van den Berg, C. E., Varoglu, A. K., & Sigri, U. (2007). Accepting death in the military: A Turkish-Dutch comparison. *International Journal of Intercultural Relations, 31*(3), 299-315. doi:10.1016/j.ijintrel.2006.05.003

Sormanti, M., & August, J. (1997). Parental bereavement: Spiritual connections with deceased children. *American Journal of Orthopsychiatry, 67*(3), 460-469. doi:http:// dx.doi.org/10.1037/h0080247

Southgate, D. E., & Roscigno, V. J. (2009). The impact of music on childhood and adolescent achievement. *Social Science Quarterly (Wiley-Blackwell), 90*(1), 4-21. Retrieved from EBSCOhost Database.

Sparkles, S. (n.d.). Retrieved from http://www.livelifehappy.com

Spellman, W. M. (2014). *A brief history of death.* London, GB: Reaktion Books.
Retrieved from Proquest Ebrary, June 3, 2016.

Steffen, E., & Coyle, A. (2010). Can 'sense of presence' experiences in bereavement be conceptualised as spiritual phenomena? Mental Health, Religion & Culture, 13(3), 273-291. doi:10.1080/13674670903357844

Stetz, M. C., McDermott, H. H., Brumage, M. R., Holcombe, P. A., Folen, R. A., & Steigman, I. (2012). Psychological distress in the military and mindfulness based training. *International Journal of Psychology Research, 7*(5), 471-484. Retrieved from https://login.libproxy.edmc.edu/login?url=http://search.proquest.com/docview/1727485039?accountid=34899

Storytelling, journaling bring comfort from grief. (2015, May 16). *Buffalo News.*
Retrieved from https://login.libproxy.edmc.edu/login?url=http://

search.proquest.com/docview/16   81113608?
accountid=34899

Strang, P. (2014). What is extreme death anxiety
and what are its consequences? *Journal
of Palliative care, 30*(4), 321-326. Retrieved
from   https://login.libproxy.edmc.edu/login?
url=http://search.proquest.com/docview/16
40765618?accountid=34899

Stroebe, M., Schut, H., & Boerner, K.
(2010). Continuing bonds in adaptation to
bereavement: Toward theoretical integration.
Clinical Psychology Review, 30(2), 259-268.
doi:10.1016/j.cpr.2009.11.007

The Buffalo News. (2015). Storytelling, journaling
bring comfort from grief. Retrieved
from   http://buffalonews.com/2015/05/16/
storytelling-journaling-bring-comfort- from-
grief/

Thomson, P. (2010). Loss and
disorganization from an attachment
perspective. *Death Studies, 34*(10), 893-914.
doi:10.1080/07481181003765410

Tyson, L. (1999). *Critical theory today: A user-*

friendly guide. New York, NY: Garland Publishing. pp. 13-32.

Tullis Owen, J. A., McRae, C., Adams, T. E., & Vitale, A. (2009). Truth troubles. *Qualitative Inquiry, 15*(1), 178-200. doi:10.1177/1077800408318316

U.S. Department of Defense. (2008). *The changing profile of the army 1985-2008.*Alexandria, VA: Author.

Vicedo, M. (2011). The social nature of the mother's tie to her child: John Bowlby's theory of attachment in post-war America. *British Journal for the History of Science, 44*(3), 401-426. doi:http://dx.doi.org/10.1017/S0007087411000318

Walsh, K., King, M., Jones, L., Tookman, A., & Blizard, R. (2002). Spiritual beliefs may affect outcome of bereavement: Prospective study. BMJ: *British Medical Journal, 324*(7353), 1551. Doi:http://dx.doi.org/10.1136/bmj.324.7353.1551

Walsh, R. N. (1990). *The spirit of shamanism.* Jeremy P. Tarcher, New York, NY. Webb, M. (1997). *The good death: The new American search to reshape* *the end of life.*New York, NY: Bantam Books.

Wiebe, E., Durepos, G., & Mills, A. J. (2010). *Encyclopedia of Case Study Research.* Los Angeles, CA: SAGE.

Worden, W. (2008). *Grief counseling and grief therapy* (4th ed.). New York, US: Springer Publishing Company. ProQuest ebrary. Retrieved May 6, 2016.

Yalom, I. (1980). *Existential psychotherapy.* New York, NY: Basic Books.

Yalom, I. (1989). *Love's executioner: And other tales of psychotherapy.* New York, NY: Basic Books.